LIVING AND GROWING IN THE OVERFLOW

SHARON GASKIN

ISBN 979-8-88943-715-4 (paperback)
ISBN 979-8-88943-717-8 (hardcover)
ISBN 979-8-88943-716-1 (digital)

Christian Faith Publishing
832 Park Avenue
Meadville, PA 16335
www.christianfaithpublishing.com

Printed in the United States of America

Contents

Introduction
The Purpose of Life

I can do all things through Christ which strengtheneth me.
—Philippians 4:13 KJV

Everyone has a purpose in life, and the purpose is to fulfill God's plans in his or her life. I'm speaking to the born-again believer who accepted Jesus Christ as his or her personal savior (Romans 10:9 NIV), in whom God purposely planted a special seed to grow in their own time. Just like a natural seed, before it gets planted in the ground, the land must be cultivated, then it will grow in its own time and season. Each seed has its own time to grow and to be harvested. When nurtured with water, good soil, and sunlight, it will grow into a mature matter. Speaking in a spiritual realm, the element is the same. To be cultivated in the Spirit, you need to read and study the Word of God daily, pray and seek his will for your life and govern yourself around believers, who will help you grow into the purpose you were called to be. Proverbs 13:20 KJV says, "He that walketh with wise men shall be wise: but a companion of fools shall be destroyed." You can stifle your growth if you do not yield to the Holy Spirit. Living, growing, flowing, and knowing his will is simple. When it comes fully developed, then you will know your purpose and growth. Once you have grown into a mature person and fully blossomed, it is time to shine. Then you shall give God all the glory that is due to him.

Stages of Life

Let's look at the stages of life—infant, toddler, child, teen adolescent, adult, middle-aged adult, and senior. As we notice, each stage of life must be developed, then we go to the next stage of life.

We cannot be a toddler who wants to go back to be an infant, crying for a bottle of milk and eating baby food that's made for an infant. The growth is no longer there; it has passed on. The toddler stage now needs more nutrition to grow and build stronger bone and muscles. A toddler should be experiencing unfamiliar words, so he or she can get more knowledge, take on new challenges and adapt new skills and behaviors. Their physical growth will be developing tremendously. Intellectual, social, and emotional changes will also develop, then they will be getting ready for the next stage in life.

During the child stage, he or she cannot take on the role of a teenager trying to drive a car or do what a teenager normally does when they are not developed in the mind yet. They will try if you let them, but it will bring on a huge responsibility for them and you. The limb should be developing unto a new growth. They should be more cognitive and more emotional. Language and speech skills should be developed, and their social development should be guided by their parents or guardians. A child should experience how to be responsible for small tasks in life. They should do chores around the house, learn to save and spend money wisely, and enjoy their childhood or youth. Once they do, they will be ready for the next stage in life.

Teen adolescence is a tender stage that needs to be protected and watched closely because some want to grow up too fast and not enjoy their youth. During the teenager stage, he or she cannot take on the role of an adult. They are not developed in the mind to make wise decisions. Not saying that some are not matured enough. You can find some teenagers that are incredibly wise and mature, but remember, that they must have the right credentials to sign important documents and to take on huge responsibility. A teenager should experience how to be responsible for large tasks in life, getting their driver's license, finding a part-time job, learning how to balance school and job while enjoying their youth.

What about a senior trying to act like a teenager, dressing and hanging around them and even talking like them? Well, first, it looks ridiculous and inappropriate. They should be setting an example for them. All because they do not want to accept that they are getting older. Being around different age groups does not make you that age. Christian seniors should be more experienced in life. They should listen to the younger generation. When they ask for advice, they should give them wise godly counsel. Christian seniors also need to show and teach them how to overcome heartaches and pain when they occur in their lives. Proverbs 22:6 NIV tells us to "start children off on the way they should go, and even when they are old, they will not turn from it." Helping the younger generation on biblical knowledge will help take the torch of God's words to the next level in life.

When we take on the wrong stage in life, then we are pushing against or toward the cycles of life. Each stage of life must come and go. We cannot go back or forward. We must act and grow where we are, so do not get stuck in a stage where you do not belong. Thank God for where you are and live to improve and become a better you.

Anything that's not working with the nature of life that God put in place is working against itself. So should the nature of our body, soul, and spirit should form in the right season and time in life. When we look at the nature of life, it formed in obedience to God's will. Flowers bloom and fade. The sun and moon rises and sets at a given time, and the earth rotates on its axis.

What a mighty God we serve, who says in Isaiah 55:11 KJV, "So shall my word be that goeth forth out of my mouth: it shall not return unto me void, but it shall accomplish that which I please, and it shall prosper in the thing whereto I sent it."

Giving—Blessing
This Is Not My Last

Study: "For God so loved the world, that he gave his only begotten Son, that whosoever believeth in him should not perish, but have everlasting life" (John 3:16 KJV).

Giving is one of God's greatest love. We shall give because he first gave to us.

I know it is hard to give when you think it is your last. I have been there, giving seems like where is my sort coming from if I give my last? How am I going to make my ends meet? You only give according to what you have, not your last. We tend to associate giving with money only, but it's more than that. I know the saying money solves all problems. Money does touch a great part of our needs. But keep in mind giving your *time, talent, faith,* and *resources* is just as important and valuable, and it plays a big part in everyone lives.

Let's talk about giving, for God loves a cheerful giver. It pleases God, and it is right in the sight of God. According to him, "Each man should give what he has decided in his heart to give, not reluctantly or under compulsion" (2 Corinthians 9:7 NIV). At some point in our lives, we will be a givers or takers. I do not know about not giving. It makes you feel good to help someone in need. It brings on a sense for rejoicing and giving praises knowing it is coming from the Lord. Pray about what you will want God to use you; you will get your answer.

Who would not serve a God like that—someone who gave his only begotten son, that whoever believes in him shall not perish but have an everlasting life (John 3:16 NIV)? *Wow,* what a God!

Believing is all that it takes. Yes, believe, but how do you believe? First, in your heart, ask God to help you believe. Let's look at Mark 9:23–24 KJV. It's about the father of a demon-possessed boy. "Jesus said unto him, If thou canst believe, all things are possible to him that believeth." The father said, "I believe; help thou mine unbelief." The father wanted the unbelief to be removed from his thought, which was when he cried out to Jesus for help. That was when the miracle took place, then his son was healed. It was like Nicodemus who asked Jesus how you can be born again; can they enter a second time into their mother's womb? "No," Jesus replied, "no one can enter the kingdom of God unless they are born of water and Spirit. Flesh gives birth to flesh, but the Spirit gives birth to spirit" (John 3:3–6 NIV). So if we want to believe on the living God—Jesus—we must pray and believe in the Spirit. And the Spirit will give birth to spirit so you can understand the kingdom of God.

God will do the same thing for us too. Remember Elijah; he was sent to Zarephath, where a widow woman and her son was living, and she thought that was the last meal for her and her son, but little did she know that God sustained her and her son because of her obedience. She gave to the man of God. He will also do the same for you and me. Read this widow's story fully on 1 Kings 17:8–16 NIV.

Sometime later, the widow's son died; she had to rely again on the man of God. The Lord heard Elijah's cry, and the boy's life returned to him, and he lived. Read this on 1 Kings 17:17–24 NIV. God heard the saints' voice when we cry out to him, so Elijah and the widow gave what they had, by being obedient to the voice of the Lord.

"Taker" people do not know how to stop. Having too much of everything is not good for you. How can you enjoy it when you have too much? You will forget that you have it. You will say, "I did not know that I had this. When did I buy it?" Now it is old and corrupted, so you will have to throw it away. Why not enjoy giving it away before it gets too worn-out? You will have a sense of joy knowing that you made another person smile.

Take an inventory before you purchase anything else, especially if you must make more room to store the added items that you bought. I like what the songwriter had said, "I'd rather have Jesus than riches, houses, and land." That is so true. What does it gain to possess all that you have and cannot enjoy it fully? You only can drive one car at a time, live in one place at a time, so enjoy helping others who are less fortunate than you.

Now the faith of the father of the demon-possessed boy grew stronger than anything was possible if he just believed. Like Nicodemus, he needed more resources, and more clarity about the kingdom of God, so the knowledge he had can help others, and the widow did not have monetary gifts to give. But she stepped out in faith in what she had. They gave what they had by putting their trust in God. And he had given it back to them in accordance to their faith.

God can honor our blessing as long we are giving from our hearts.

Supporter—Encourager
Blessing Beyond Measure

Study: As Ruth was with Naomi (Ruth 4:15 NIV)

Are you a supporter of something different from yourself? We all support ourselves on any occasion. Like for instance, you support yourself where you live, where you shop, and where to go on vacation, so let us look at the whole picture. If you are, that is great, because you're supposed to love yourself first before you can love anyone else.

Ruth is one of the prime examples of a supporter. She supported her mother-in-law, Naomi, to the fullest and look how God had blessed her by being a supporter to someone she loved dearly. She knew the inconvenience she was facing—living a new life, changing the custom from serving an idol god to a living God, learning the new custom of working in the field, which she probably had never done before. She had to be taught how to glean, how to gather, where to stay, and who to follow (Ruth 2:8 KJV). Being a supporter will pay off.

Ruth knew her heart was saying, "Go with mother-in-law, Naomi, to encourage her and give her some support." Naomi thought Ruth was just talking because of the sorrow she had for her. But Ruth's actions spoke louder than her words.

Naomi did not know the plan of God. She tried to stop Ruth from coming with her. Sometimes we can mess up our blessing by trying to stop people from supporting us. We think it is a handout, a charity case. It is far from the truth, and we let our pride get in the way. Proverbs 16:18 NIV tells us that "pride goes before destruction, a haughty spirit before a fall." So you do not want your pride to get in the way, because there comes the fall.

We are told that when there's a fire, we should *stop*, *drop*, and roll, which will protect us from any harm. So I am saying this: "When things get heated in our life, we need to listen carefully, think about what we heard, and pray earnestly for the answer." So *listen*, *think*, and *pray*. This is the spiritual medicine that I am taking as well. We should ask God for clarity when we are not sure of what action to take.

Do you know anybody you can support? Are there any charity organizations you can help? I give to Goodwill, and I shop at Goodwill. When you shop there, you are supporting that organization. Many people shop at Goodwill but do not even know that they are helping that organization. Meal on Wheels, which feeds the older adults and children, is a good organization. There are so many organizations out there. Pick one that piques you, and you will have a sense of helping other people in need.

For some reason, Ruth had a strong bond with her mother-in-law, and nothing was going to stop her from coming. She knew they both needed to encourage each other at this time of sorrow. Read Ecclesiastes 4:9–10 NIV.

Once Naomi gave in on the persuasion of Ruth coming, that's when the blessing began. Remember Ruth was young, and she was able to supply the food for them. Naomi did not have to work. Ruth went out into the field to gather the food for her and Naomi, which was a blessing. In today's world, someone is working on a job, and you are staying home, and the provider comes home with the food and other essential items that you need. What a blessing! And Ruth knew how to bless her elder and give them respect. Ruth respected Naomi in everything she taught her by being respectful and trusting her wise counsel. Ruth took Naomi's advice on how to conduct herself around Boaz, and that gave Ruth honor and blessing through Boaz's love. So Ruth was a supporter of her mother-in-law, Naomi. I believe Naomi had given Ruth respect also, while she was married to her son. Mahlon. That's why their bond was so rich in spirit. Ruth came to be a great blessing. Getting married to the rich man Boaz and having his child, Obed, not just any child, but the child of the genealogy of Jesus Christ (Matthew 1:5 NIV).

Giving Naomi a blessing beyond measure in her old age, which she thought never would come, blessed Ruth so highly that her life and favor were richly blessed that her joy was completed.

Now since we had proven that, let us go out and support and encourage someone.

Helper—Assistant
Angels in Disguise

Study: "God is our refuge and strength" (Psalm 46:1 KJV).

We have said this many times, "I will only help if they help themselves." We've all been there. But the truth is, it is written in the Word of God to help. We must decide by the Holy Spirit to know when and where to help and not be a hindrance. By showing them what help is about and how to take the torch to help others, I believe they will have the same feeling of gratitude as you did when you came to help with their needs. It is God's way of showing his love to them.

Sometimes we cannot see the hand of God helping us, but he is, and sometimes we can. Even when we are not in his will, he is still there to help us if only we could imagine how he watches over us every day as a parent watches over their children. Living under God's umbrella is amazing. You do get scared, but that is okay. It a natural feeling.

Just keep on praying in the Spirit when you are feeling uneasy at times.

You can find more people than you know who love to help and assist others when it is needed. You will be surprised, but my thing is, do they know how their help matters to other people? Do they know their impact, or the course they made to someone's life? And sometimes, you find people only helping people whom they want to help. It amazes me to see how they do not have any conscience at all. Believe me, God sees everything that is done in secret (Ecclesiastes 12:13–14 KJV).

It once was said, it takes a village to raise a family, but sad to say, the world is getting so cold that Christians have a nonchalant Spirit—like, this is what's owed to me. I do not need God. I did it myself. If you call on God's name, people get offended and offensive (SMH). Let's get back to our places and be who God wants us to be, soldiers in the army of the Lord.

If you see your brother or sister in the Lord fall short, it is more right to help them up. We all fall short in the glory of the Lord (Romans 3:23 NIV). But if that person does not want to be restored in their rightful place, the best alternative is to pray for him or her. They cannot stop you for praying for them. Only if they knew the love you have for them, they will be surprised. It is with the grace and unmeasured favor from God above that is working in your born-again Spirit, which allows you to love unconditionally.

The helpers are people who spend hours in school learning a skill on how to help others. These are some of the helpers—doctors, nurses, lawyers, teachers, and many more. Advocates and speakers are other types of helpers. Let's talk about the quicker helper in need. For example, someone had a flat, and you came to help them in their need of stress to fix their tire. That time and resources that you took out to help, you will never get it back again. You cannot turn back the time and the energy you gave to someone in their need. But keep in mind that God sees every kind deed you have shown and sown in a person's life, and he is going to reward you for your kind help. Someone let's you get in front of them when the traffic is in a jam to avoid any accident; that is a helper. You only have a few items, but the line in the grocery store is long, so someone gives you favor to get in front of them; that is a helper. Your finances are low, so they come to your rescue in a time of need; that is a helper.

I call them the angels in disguise because they always go around looking for someone in need of help, trying to find some way to lend a helping hand and offer what they can do. They are always around at the right time when you need them. They also volunteer their time to support and help others in need.

God always has special children whom he had formed on the earth to be a helper and to assist others. Sometimes it is an actual angel from above (Acts 5:15 KJV).

Let's be a helper and assist others in need.

Unforgiveness—Resentment
You Are a Child of God

Study: "I say not unto thee until seven times" (Matthew 18:22 KJV).

It is good that Jesus's disciples asked him a lot of questions. That's how we learn, being inquisitive. Some people may call it being nosy, but I like the word *inquisitive* because you do not know unless you ask. At the beginning of Matthew chapter 18, the disciples were asking questions. "Who is the greatest in the kingdom of heaven?" Jesus had to give them an example by calling a little child unto him, giving them a prime example. They saw, and heard what Jesus was teaching them. They were questioning him daily and finding all sources of answers, not the answer they were looking for but an answer from above. Now we go to the question of whether they knew that they had right. Should we forgive them seven times? Jesus answered, "No, but seventy times seven." So who is counting seventy times seven? I do not believe anyone will be counting on how many times someone has offended them. We do not even count right at the bat. Once it is over, we are done. Jesus is letting us know that people are going to offend us, so we must forgive them in Jesus's name and go on. Once we place it in him, we can let go. He got it.

I know the saying on this one too. I can forgive, but I cannot forget. If we stop thinking about it, we might eventually forget it too. Why not forgive? What do you have to lose? Oh, I know. You'll lose resentment, pain, headache, sorrow, misery, and discomfort. You know, those things you hate to lose, you enjoy their company. Please do not leave. Stay here and make me more miserable. You have gotten so accustomed to it that it got you so bonded from yourself. You are so embedded in your thinking, so deeply embedded that you are like drowning in quicksand. All I can say is the person who hurt you so deeply is a person working for Satan and not of God. Or that person has no idea that he or she is hurting you. I know the hurt can be so strong especially coming from a family member or someone that you really look up to. All I know is that person has a different spirit working through them at that time when the hurt began. We cannot change it. It is already done, so we need to stop pondering over the hurt and give it to God, so the healing can start taking place. And it will also help our physical healing process as well.

When you are feeling unforgiveness and resentment toward someone, your whole appearance changes. You look like you are mad at the entire world because of what that person or someone had said or done. You cannot become a productive citizen because you are still stuck in the past and cannot go forward. They do not have the last word. Really you do. I know you heard this many times because we have all heard it. Forgiveness is not for them. It is for you. We are giving them more power than they deserve. Now you know you do not want to give anyone more power than yourselves, especially if it's not of good will.

What does God say about who you are? You are a child of God (John 1:12 KJV). No weapon formed against you shall prosper (Isaiah 54:17 NIV). If we speak these words daily, all form of unforgiveness will cease because we remind ourselves of who we are, and no one can change that.

Pray for that person who did you wrong, then ask the Lord if you need to confront the person. If you have peace, go to that person. You will be surprised that the person needs to ask you for your forgiveness too. You will be able to cherish that moment. Joy will overflow, and that will be another chapter that you can close. If you get offended in life again, then you will have more compassion for that person and will pray for them.

Setting boundaries is okay. Being around positive people is good, it's not that you will never get hurt but keep trusting in the Lord. Continue saying positive words of God daily, so unforgiveness and resentment can change into forgiveness and contentment.

Love—Affection
Help Me, Holy Spirit

Study: "*Love one* another as I have loved you" (John 13:34 NIV).

God's love is free. It does not cost any money or action from us for God to grant his free love toward us. It takes place first in the spiritual realm.

He paid it all. The payment of love is paid in full. It never diminishes; the love grows stronger and stronger as we walk closer to him.

It's been known that some people do not know how to receive and give genuine love. They must be taught how to accept the care of others. Once they do, there is a window of opportunity for them. Then they will have a broader spectrum of life in the future.

Here is some of the type of love we should acquire from the Lord—*philia* (affectionate love, brotherly love), *storge* (familiar love), *eros* (romantic love, married love), and *agape* (God's love for humankind).

It amazes me when you give people advice to help them in their daily lives. Some run with it and take the advice, while some ponder and think that you do not know what you are talking about. Or you are out to get them, you do not want the best for them. I know because it came from you. Some people do not receive what you have to say but let someone else that they do not even know say the exact information, and they will receive it gladly and with joy. I know that it is not just me who goes through the same things.

Corrected criticism can hurt, but it is the best love that anyone can give, only if you are advising with the love of God. Eventually, they will realize that your love really matters to them and not to harm them.

This is a familiar passage that everyone—I believe—has heard whether they are a Christian or not (it easier said than done to give genuine affectionate love). Or I only love someone if they love me back; that is the only way that I can love you. To me, it seems like they have their guard up and are afraid to let it down, and if they do, they think they will get hurt. Or they've been hurt before and dare not take a second chance. Only with the grace of God and as a new creature you are in Christ, it will be done. You cannot love based on feeling, which is the nature, but by his grace and his unmeasurable power, you can love like God.

We all interpret love in a different matter, but true love comes from God. If we can follow and appear in the Spirit of God through the Holy Spirit, we can break the yoke of hatred, envy, and jealousy. The Bible tells us that hatred is a liar (see 1 John 4:20 KJV). Jealousy and envy are enemies of the soul, and Scripture warns us against them over and over. We are told that jealousy and envy are fruits of the flesh (see Galatians 5:21 NIV), an antonym of love (see 1 Corinthians 13:4 NIV), a symptom of pride (see 1 Timothy 6:4 NIV), a catalyst for conflict (see James 3:16 NIV), and a mark of unbelievers (see Romans 1:29 NIV). The only right way to respond is to repent, turning from the poison of our envy, hatred, and jealousy by looking at the source and asking the Holy Spirit for some help. We cannot do it on our own, but with God's help, it can be done. It is written in the book of Genesis how jealousy and hatred can ruin a family, the first family. Cain was so angry and jealous of Abel's offering that his countenance fell. God had said to Cain, "If thou do well, shalt thou are not accepted (Genesis 4:7 KJV). So that tells me it is all up to us to do what is right, and love will prevail.

If you are harboring hatred, malice, or grudge toward your brother and sister in the Lord, the healing or breakthrough for you or your family will not be released for you. How can you pray for others if you are holding on to these unwanted spirits? Do not give your offering, go, and make amends with them, so your offering can be accepted by God (Matthew 5:24 NIV). Then you will find blessing and no curse, healing and no pain, joy and no sorrow.

We also can study the book of Nehemiah. Nehemiah was assigned to repair the temple of Jerusalem, which God appointed him to do, and he got permission from the king to go ahead to repair the wall. Nehemiah was not letting negative people from the outside to disturb him and the worker who was helping him in preparing the wall as many tried to stop the progress from being completed.

However it did not hinder or persuade Nehemiah to stop. Once you know that God agrees, you can rest for sure it will get done.

Remember that *love always wins*.

Patience—Waiting
Living on God's Timing

Study: "Support the weak be patient toward all men" (1 Thessalonians 5:14 KJV).

Being patient is one of my biggest problems even today. It is like a thorn in my flesh. Let me tell you a little story. I have more, but this is the most recent one.

God must set the Holy Spirit before us. Do not go before him. If we go before him, we will lose out. I was once in line to get my oil change and brand-new tires for my car. Very impatient was I; some people were in line before me. The only thing I could think of was getting out of line and going somewhere else. You know—getting out of this line to go and stand in another line—that's absurd. Remember I had to drive to another car shop, and that will be some time spent. Wow, impatient was I, all because it was my day off. By the time I was done waiting, I received discounts upon discounts. Waiting and being patient is very important. It is the trick of the enemy when you don't wait on the Lord. We proceed to do things our way. Note that in everything in life, waiting is a must because God's timing is different from ours. Oh yes, by the way, he made time.

During that time of waiting, I was praying for patience. I did learn that, later that day, you might meet someone, or God has you there to minister to someone who may be lost or need some encouragement, which could be you too! I met someone who knows Father God. We talked about God and his *grace* and mercy and how his protection is all around us. Just think, this precious child of God—I would have missed her had I let my impatience take over. I cherished that moment with her. We might meet again. Who knows, but I do know she encouraged me while she was there at that moment. Father God, thank you for the time I spent with her.

Sometimes if we feel we are getting too impatient, it will be easy to stop and take a deep breath and start praying in the Spirit and singing melody in your heart to the Lord. It will help.

We have to realize that God's time is not our time, and that waiting on something is not in God's making yet. If we rush to get it, it will not be developed in our mind to keep it, or it is not what God wants us to have. He knows what is best for us.

Being impatient, like driving in a hurry, to get to where you want to be, please slow down because, you know, that will cause an accident or get you a ticket. Look at the whole picture; you are going to make it. Even though you may be late, that was the time that was chosen for you, but you do not want to be extra late by getting into an accident or getting a ticket.

Patience is a virtue. (Faith, hope, charity are characteristics of virtue.) What are you waiting on? During the time you are waiting, read one of my favorite verses, Psalm 27:14 KJV, "Wait on the Lord: be of good courage, and he shall strengthen thine heart: wait, I say, on the Lord." Do not only wait on the Lord but be in a good attitude. Take note that he is going to answer your request.

The psalms also said it twice—to wait lets you know to be patient. It is going to happen in his timing, and it's going to be on time.

During the time that I was waiting for my answer from the Lord, God answered my request, not the time that I was looking for, but it was answered on his time. So if we believe in our heart and don't waver in our faith, then our request will be granted. Also, Abram believed God, and it was credited to him as righteousness. Study Genesis 15:6 NIV.

Abraham was one of whom God promised a son, which he said he would do, even when Sarai, his wife, persuaded him to have a child by her handmaid, Hagar; Abram agreed (Genesis 16:1–2 KJV) and had the child of the bondwoman. God still promised Abraham and Sarah a son in their old age, the child of promise—Isaac (Galatians

4:28)—from the free woman, so we are children of the promise and heir of the free woman, which was God's time for us (Galatians 4:29–31 KJV).

So if you are feeling doubt about your situation, believe God's word on what he will do. He is the same today as he was yesterday. His words do not go out void. "He is a rewarder of them that diligently seek him" (Hebrews 11:6 KJV). With God, all things are possible.

Happiness—Contentment
Trying Something New

Study: "Blessed is the man that walketh not in the counsel of the ungodly" (Psalm 1:1 KJV)

Finding happiness and contentment is not hard; all we must do is think on the goodness of God. Let's look at some simple happiness in the Lord—for example, cooking, think of the ingredients, how it was formed by God, the outcome of the recipe you are making; sewing, the fabric material, the softness, the texture, how it was created; walking or running; being out in the sunlight or moonlight; dancing; singing; and playing the instrument. Trivial things we may take for granted can show up to bring in happiness and contentment.

You may think that is just going through the routine of everyday life, which is nothing new. So what? How can that bring me some happiness? When you go on a deeper thought of who made everything, before the world was formed, God called everything forth—from the darkness to the light, setting the moon, star, and sun in place. Everything was formed by God for us to accomplish here on earth. Then God said go out and be fruitful and multiply not only with children, but be fruitful in your creativity—a new dish, which was created by you; new dress or suit, new song. That should bring on some happiness. And if you do not create it, improve it.

It is a shame that when you want the best for a particular person that you know, that person only thinks you are a threat to him or her. They think everything you do is out to get them, or you do not want them to be happy. You try, and you try hard to convince them that you care for them and hope for the best in their lives. But your actions are to no avail because they think the worst in you. Little do they know it is the enemy within themselves; they need to do a reverse role by stepping out and looking within themselves, to find out what is the problem. If that person is giving you some good advice and knowledge that helps you in any way, wow, that person is not your enemy. It is someone that cares and knows the Lord and wants the best in your life. Go in prayer and ask the Lord to take away that stubborn spirit of rejection so you can find happiness and contentment.

We should not wait on someone to make us happy. Happiness comes in all distinct types of form. What do I mean? Come on now, we must think outside of the box. Like I said above, there's sewing, cooking, dancing, singing, and playing the instrument. We can create new ideas on all that I name. If you do not know how to sew, try it. I bet you laugh. Start with something small like a pot holder. I bet you will be amazed on what you had created, and there comes the laugher. You don't have to do something to fulfill your happiness. Until all your projects are gone, then you will be feeding on the next project.

Try to look on the positive side of life. If someone comes to you with a sad story—for example, it's been raining all day. You say yes, but the sun is going to shine again. I do not have enough money to buy this dress and shoe. You say yes, but one day you will have enough money to buy three dresses and three pairs of shoes. Give them the positive side of life. So they can be content on whatever they have. That will give them hope even if they do not see it yet. Do not take on negative problems. We have enough of them already. Once we start speaking, the opposite of the negative situation will turn. Our words are powerful. "Death and life are in the power of the tongue" (Proverbs 18:21 KJV).

Once we learn to be happy ourselves, then it will be contagious to others. Keep in mind that you are feeding on your emotion, but it is only going to last for a moment. Joy often succeeds in happiness. Joy comes from God, and it will last forever.

Someone made a statement when you are feeling down or sad about something, just start smiling. Turn that frown into a smile even if you do not feel like it. Try it and see what will happen. You have nothing to lose but a frown.

Hope—Expectation
Looking for a Better Outcome

Study: "Now faith is the substance of things hoped for" (Hebrews 11:1 KJV).

Hope is something that you do not see, but believe that it will happen. It is a feeling of expectation and desire for a certain thing to happen. What are you hoping for—good health, financial blessing, new vehicle? Everyone hopes even when they are just saying the actual word *hope*, and not even realizing that they are using God's instruction of faith.

I hope this day will be a better day than yesterday, or I hope tomorrow will be a better day. Hope is good. It lets us know we are using faith because we do not know what tomorrow holds, but God does. So when we say hope in a sentence, we go by faith and expectation. I hope I get this job. I hope she or he will get better. I hope my money will come soon. Ha ha, I know I will get you on that one, so let's put God in the equation. God, I hope this will be a better day. God, I hope she or he will get better. God, I hope I get the job. Trusting and believing in things and by putting God first is the right and most important thing we can do. It is honoring God first, putting him before all areas of our life.

God is our defender. Once we call on him, then he has full access to the problem. He sends his angel ahead of the situation. Then we must do our part of being *hopeful* and patient. It reminds me of the book of Daniel 10:1–21 NIV where Michael the angel was sent to help another angel, who was held up by honoring Daniel's request. One chapter ahead in chapter 9 was the turning point. So anytime we confess our sin and surrender and seriously and honestly pray to the living God, he will answer us. Daniel confessed his sin and the sin of his people. Study Daniel 9:20–23 NIV. God hears us, and he honors our prayers. Remember that our prayer can be held up. The angel told Daniel from the first day that he prayed, his prayer was honored, but he was held up for twenty-one days by the prince of the kingdom of Persia. The angel himself had to call the chief angel, Michael, to come and intervene. So our prayer can be held up not because of something we have done wrong or because we did not do this or that. As long as we are in his will, keeping his name embedded in our hearts and minds and being Christlike, no work is involved in it. Just keep believing by asking God for help. Keep in mind that sometimes our prayer has been answered, yet we do not even see it. So examine your prayer request closely, take the blinder off, and study it carefully and see if it has been answered. Once it had been answered, that's when the praises go up, and God get all the glory that is due to him. Hallelujah!

Hagar, Sarai's handmaid, found hope in the Lord. After Sarai treated her harshly, which made her fled from the land where she was living, Hagar cried out in the wilderness on the road to Egypt. She was expecting a miracle to take place. The Lord heard her cry; she called the place El Roi, the God who sees me. She returned home and bore Abram a son, and Abram gave the name Ishmael (Genesis 16:14–15 NIV).

Remember, every problem has a solution to it. The right and wrong choices we make in life can harm or bless us. Take a closer look and examine your outcome because it is going to come back in full circle. When choosing the right one, you will never fall.

Just remember that there is hope and expectation in every situation, no matter how doomed and dull the problem may look or seem. The sun is going to shine again; just hold on and do not faint. In just a little while longer, you will see your breakthrough.

God sees you when you cry out to him, so go to God when you are in need (Psalm 40:1 KJV).

Holy One Pray Earnestly—the acronym for HOPE.

Peace—Calmness
Speaking to Things Too

Study: "Peace, I leave with you; my peace I give you" (John 14:27 KJV).

Shalom, Shalom, Shalom—that is my middle name in the spiritual realm. There's nothing like peace, I know. I am being realistic. I know in the world we are going to have trials and tribulations because we are living in a fallen world, and we know it is going to be chaos, and many more are to come, but for real, it can be peaceful and calm, most of the time, even with a large group of people.

This brings my attention to when Jesus calmed the sea. "Peace, be still." That is impressive to speak to a thing and tell it to be still—what power and authority! So what do you think? Read Mark 4:35–41 KJV. Wow, that is impressive. Just think, the sea was cutting up, the wind blowing hard, water getting into the boat, the boat rocking back and forth. And Jesus was sleeping, was not bothered about anything until his disciples woke him up, asking, "Teacher, do you not care if we drown?"

His disciples were astonished hearing and seeing the reaction to his word and how the sea came to be obedient to him. They were firsthand witness of the miracle that took place. They also saw many other blessing and healing during their time they spent with Jesus, being taught by Jesus. They learned how to do what he did, walk where he walked, talk how he talked, and pray how he prayed even when their faith got smaller. He had to discipline them on their faith "O, ye of little faith?" (Luke 12:28 KJV).

You spoke to things too—when your car would not start. "Come on and start, please," and it started; when you are running late, "Please, Lord, stop the clock," and you made it on time. "Thank God, I made it on time." "I need this call." You hope for the phone to ring. "Please ring," and the phone rang in thirty minutes to give you the answer that you were waiting for. We are speaking things into existence when things go wrong. We want peace and calm. We sometimes do not use the word *peace*, but we want peace.

Live at peace with all men (Romans 12:18 NIV). To me, it is saying try not to start any argument, disagreement, fight, disheartenment, hatred, or rebellion. It is a spirit from the devil himself. This is what it's like. Just wait until I get my hand on him or her. I don't want them asking me for anything. They want hear the last of this. We can go on and on. I've been there. This will stunt your growth in the Lord, and the problem is, how long do you want to stay there? I want to serve the living God that my father Abraham, Isaac, and Jacob served. And my earthly father and mother also served. If we use the opposite of disagreement, fight, disheartenment, hatred, and similar words, there will be peace.

Every trials and tribulations is a test. We are going to fail or pass it. It is up to the individuals on their score of what they make. If we look at it that way, we will want a better score. Hold your words before you speak. Everything is not speedily to say something all the time.

There is going to be a day that we are going to lie down with the animal, and no harm will come to us, like before when Adam and Eve were living (Genesis 2:10 NIV) peacefully on earth and in the beautiful garden of Eden. Just in my imagination, the garden of Eden looks like a painting on a canvas, just adorable, breathtaking rivers to look at—Pishon, Gihon, Hiddekel, and Euphrates. They supply all the nutrition that the land needs, fresh and refreshing to humans, animals, birds, and nature.

Looking at the flowers and nature today is lovely, but think of the flowers, mountains, and rivers that have never been corrupted. We know in the Word that it said, it is coming back again (Revelation 22:1–21 NIV). Eden restored, hallelujah! Thank God, we are coming back home, where there's supposed to be peace and calm on earth at last. No harm comes to anyone. We all can lay down with the wild animals, and be at peace.

"Peace I leave with you" (John 14:27 KJV).

Joy—Happiness
Singing Melody in Our Heart

Study: "For his anger endureth but a moment" (Psalm 30:5 KJV)

Think on the glory of the Lord and meditate in the Spirit.

I have focused on the beginning of this verse, but the whole verse is inspired by God when King David wrote, "For his anger endured but a moment; in his favor is life" (Psalm 30:5 KJV). "But do not forget this one thing, dear friends: with the Lord a day is like a thousand years, and a thousand years are like a day" (2 Peter 3:8 NIV). That is impressive. We cannot even fathom or imagine a moment in God's timing—how long is a moment? Is it a blink of an eye? All we know is his time is quick, and his favor is life. Come on now. We all want favor and life. Having some moment spent with God is awesome. You know the feeling when you spend some time with your family and friends, the one that you love so dearly, that special moment that you do not want to leave. You are so happy you cherish that moment and keep it close to your heart. Having favor from above, from God, and with man, and life engages in him. It is still impressive. What a mighty God we serve.

Psalm 30:5 KJV says, "Weeping may endure for a night but joy cometh in the morning." We have all wept, felt sorry for ourselves, had a pity party, and on and on we go with our anger and the way we have been treated. Okay, I get it, but we all have hurt someone too. Now it is time to get over it. You can find *joy* in the Lord, like King David said, it's only supposed to last a night. Okay, I am not talking about nighttime. David uses the illustration of a brief period whatever your night is. I do not know, but I do know God's anger is just a moment. If we hold onto joy in the Lord, our night won't be as long; it will cease over time.

We sing the song "Joy to the World"—it seems—like only during Christmastime, but joy is renewing every morning. We have a chance to be joyful every day when we wake up. We can grab on to joy by knowing that God sent his son, Jesus Christ, for us that we can have life, and with the abundance that it brings, to receive joy that is something that was given to us through Christ because it came from him, and no one can take it from us.

It lets us know even in the midst of being hurt, disappointed, or feeling sad, we can grab onto joy by asking the Holy Spirit for some help to bring on the joy, so the hurt, disappointment, and sadness will cease in time. We must focus on the good things that the Lord says will come and start singing melodies in our hearts to take away the bad feelings. God's music has a therapeutic effect, and it will soothe your unwanted spirit. If melon can take away King Saul's spirit of unease, just think about the melon on our spirit. Do not forget about praying in the Spirit.

Joy is just a little three-letter word that is so powerful when it is used in God's term. You cannot get another word from it. That's how powerful it is; it stands alone. It calms every pain and heartache. Joy just overflows with peace. Sometimes you cannot understand it when you are going through things, and joy comes into the room. Everything ceases and flees because it will take away all those unwanted feelings that you have. If you place your care on God and leave it, then joy will take residence in your heart and mind.

Make up your own song to the Lord. I did long ago. You do not have to be a singer to sing to the Lord, which I was not gifted with. I just started giving him thanks and adoring his presence, loving him for being who he is to me. You will get a sense of joy knowing that you created a personal song to the Lord. So keep on singing your melody to the Lord. He's listening.

Kindness—Friendliness
Smiling Can Be Contagious

Study: "Be kind and compassionate to one another" (Ephesians 4:32 NIV).

Everybody is special. Everybody is somebody even if we are not known in the public eyes. We are someone in God's eyes. He made us and fashioned us in our mother's womb. He stitched us together. Just think about our unique fingerprint; no one has the same one. So you know, he thought of every one of us to be very special. And he also said he do not want anyone lost; he wanted everybody saved (2 Peter 3:9 KJV).

Being kind and friendly is not hard. We make it hard by just looking at someone and going on their looks, and we tend to not be kind. Because they did not speak to us, but did we speak to them? It does not matter who speak first because we do not know what may happen, or if we run across them again in life, if we leave a good impression, we might have favor from them. They may become your doctor, nurse, or your judge. We do not know. I try to speak to everyone even if they do not speak back. Start in the morning; saying good morning to someone would not hurt you or me. It is good to me because God has given us another day. Having another chance is good, another chance to ask for forgiveness. Just think, another chance to hug, laugh, play, see the flowers bloom in the spring, see autumn leaves in the fall when the sunlight turns orange—trivial things. I can go on and on. You know, think on some things that make you happy and joyful. So being kind to others even if we do not know that person can make a difference in their lives. They may want to tell you about their life stories; just listen to them. You may not be able to get a word in, but it is okay that all that they need is for someone just to listen to their problem. We do not know what they are going through. Your word of kindness or your smile can break the cycle and roller coaster of what they are going through.

Now you have a chance to ask them if they have accepted Jesus Christ as their personal savior. If not, introduce them to Romans 6:23 KJV. Once you all depart, finish off with a prayer.

It takes a special person to be a server or a waiter because even if they came to work upset about something, they still got to show compassion and friendliness to their customer. Anyone who works around the public must be professional on their job. Just to name a few—pastors, nurses, doctors, and teachers, many more—they are really made for their jobs even when things do not go well with the church, customers, patients, or students that they are serving. These are peculiar people with an exceptional quality or traits. That's why, it is necessary, imperative for saints to show more love, compassion, and kindness around anyone we meet than ever before (1 Peter 4:10 NIV).

Some people think they are not loved. What a smile can do in a hurting person's life, you just made their day when you initiate the smile first, and believe me, that person will know that someone does care, and they probably are smiling just about all day thinking on the smile that you had given them.

During our toddler stage, the first time we ever heard the word *be kind* was from our parents or grandparents. That word was so strong and bold coming from them. "Be kind," they will say in a sturdy voice to you or your sibling. "Stop doing that," whatever you were doing, that was wrong. You knew it was the opposite of what you were doing, so you found out the definition quickly, and in a hurry, you acted nice or else. (The toy will be taken away from you.)

You looked back at them and saw the smile on your parents' or guardians' faces, then you knew you made the right decision.

We should continue to use the word *kind* throughout our lifetime, knowing once we give kindness, it will come back to us in full circle. It will bring on a sense of repeated cycles. So keep smiling and be kind. It is very contagious.

Gentleness—Niceness
Soft and Calm Words

Study: "Gentle answer turns away wrath" (Proverbs 15:1 NIV).

A gentle and pleasant words calm the atmosphere and soothe the soul. More gentle words are much needed in times like this. Words of the wise take heart.

Sometimes, we have the intention to let the other person know just how we feel. I am going to give him or her a piece of my mind. The words we say we sometimes do not even realize it. If I keep breaking off my mind, I won't have anything for myself. I know it is a figure of speech, but sadly, it is the truth. We are breaking part of ourselves daily out into the atmosphere because once you place your word, good or bad, the seed's been planted, and it is going to cultivate to the form in which it is planted. Look at Matthew 12:36–37 KJV.

When a problem comes into our lives, we need to solve the problem quickly, so it won't fester into something larger and grow into a deeper root. "You do not have to fight your battle of defending yourself. Leave it to me," the Lord said, and "I will take care of it." So stop fighting against yourself, just ask God for a gentle and humble spirit.

Remember the little foxes that spoil the vines. Read Song of Solomon 2:13–15 NIV. Be always prayerful and watchful because your enemies, which are symbolized as little foxes, will try to destroy your vines. This will be your vines—vines of love, peace, happiness, and joy. My suggestion is to have godly people who will continue to pray for you and give you godly advice. You can continue to pray too and anoint yourself; that's where you will get your strength.

Doing things in the flesh won't accomplish anything. Two people argue over trivial issues, and no one wants to back down, so did I. I knew about Christ, but trying to manage the situation in the flesh, wouldn't work at all. You must be fully engulfed and baptized in the Holy Spirit to gain the knowledge and understanding of God's word. It is nothing magical or scary; just ask the Lord to fill you with the knowledge of the Holy Spirit. Yes, that old unwanted flesh will try to sneak back in but pray in the Spirit, and knowing the trick of the enemy always will denounce the flesh. Paul in Ephesians 6:10–18 KJV was telling the Ephesians about the armor of God, saying, "to put on the whole armor of God that ye may be able to stand against the wiles of the devil. For we wrestle…against…spiritual wickedness in high places…loins girt…with the truth…breastplate of righteousness…feet shod with the preparation of the gospel of peace…shield of faith…helmet of salvation, and the sword of the Spirit…praying always with all prayer and supplication in the Spirit." Speaking of Satan and his wickedness, it reminds me of the devil looking around to see who he might destroy among the saints of God. Job 1:6–8 NIV tells us that "Satan answered the Lord, 'From roaming throughout the earth, going back and forth on it.'" Well, you know, he's still doing his same old trick. Nothing has changed. You should not be surprised or get off course of his fictive because that's what he wants you and me to do. Stand strong and be unmovable and trust and obey the Word of God; nothing will get us off course.

It is a daily walk with the Lord. We will stumble at time, but we cannot quit. Like a surfer, once he falls off his board, he does not stop and say, "No more surfing for me. It is too hard." Instead, he goes to the wave and current of the ocean. He learns from the rise and fall and goes back at it, over and over until perfection. Someone learning to ride a bike doesn't say, "Okay, I fell off. I am going to put this bike up. I am not good at it." Instead, he did the same as the surfer. He got back on the bike and pedaled until he can hold on it steadily without falling. A swimmer doesn't say, "I am afraid of the water." Instead, he goes back swimming until his fear leaves and he can use his body to form the motion of swimming. It is a daily improvement. You keep on praying and asking God for a gentle spirit, alone with gentle love.

One day at a time, sweet Jesus, that's all we are asking from you, and one day, it will come. One day, you are going to be tempted, and that's when you are going to find out about your gentle spirit. Look at Philippians 4:13 KJV that says, "I can do all things through Christ which strengthened me."

Once you learn to have a quite spirit, it will make a world of a difference in your life. No more headache, sorrow, or pain. The other person will see the change in you and they will want to have the same change.

Standing on his word, acknowledge God's way. Trust and put all your resources to work. In the spiritual realm, it will make a difference. Gentle and nice makes a world of difference too.

Now we are *living* and *growing* in *the overflow*.

Goodness—Mercy
Good—empathy

Psalms 23:6 - "Surely goodness and mercy shall
follow me all the days of my life: and I will dwell
in the house of the LORD forever.

One might ask that trying to be good is difficult, how can one try to do something good when it's not in oneself? You go on with the motion of your daily tasks, doing something you do not want to do for others to prove to yourself that you are a good morale person and that your goodness will pay off. You are making yourself miserable and the people around you.

Smiling when a frown is in your spirit, walking away with a sense of thinking you show them with your goodness, it's time to get my reward. Remember, a believer knows when a genuine friend comes to show goodwill toward them, they can sense God's presence. Saying you are Christ-like and doing the opposite is not giving the sweet aroma that God desires. So, stop wearing the name claiming that you are a Christian, and it is far from the truth.

Handing out tracks but not reading it yourself.

You say you care but it's the opposite of hate.

You say you love but you show backbiting.

You say you give but you hold back.

You say you have empathy, but you show emptiness.

Once and for all, be true to yourself; why do you go on with this agony and pain of lying to yourself and others by being a Christian, but it is false? Stop the false attempt and set yourself free of the pain. Take off the blindness. Don't waste another day of shame; you are not hurting anyone but yourself. God can come in and perk that stony heart for a heart of flesh. Change the hate to caring, backbiting to love, give to give abundance and the emptiness to empathy. Ask God to help you in that area of goodness then you will learn how it feels to do good to someone, even someone that you do not know.

We do not want to hear the word Jesus will say to us in **Matthew 7:21 I Never Knew You.**

> 21 "Not everyone who says to me, 'Lord, Lord,' will enter the kingdom of heaven, but the one who does the will of my Father who is in heaven. 22 On that day many will say to me, 'Lord, Lord, did we not prophesy in your name, and cast out demons in your name, and do many mighty works in your name?' 23 And then will I declare to them, 'I never knew you; depart from me, you workers of lawlessness.'

Or, in our words of today, "Lord, I went to Church on Sunday, gave my tithes, visited the sick, and worked in the Christian bookstore," on with our due diligence. It's excellent if love, compassion, and empathy play a part in every role we take on.

> Matthew 5:8 NIV Blessed are the pure in heart, for they will see God.

Faithfulness—Faith
Trust—loyal

Psalm 23:4 (English Standard Version): Even though I walk through the valley of the shadow of death, I will fear no evil, for you are with me; your rod and your staff, they comfort me.

This is a familiar and pleasant chapter, as we read in God's word, "Even though I walk through the **valley of the shadow of death**." We are walking through it, not stopping but walking. Now, let's look at Valley, Shadow, and Death.

Merriam Webster Dictionary

A **valley:** an elongate depression of the earth's surface usually between ranges of hills or mountains an area drained by a river and its tributaries a low point or condition: **hollow**, **depression** the place of meeting of two slopes of a roof that forms on the plan a reentrant angle

A **Shadow** is the dark figure cast upon a surface by a body intercepting the rays from a source of light, partial darkness or obscurity within a part of space from which rays from a source of light are cut off by an interposed opaque body a small degree or portion: **trace**

A **Death:** a permanent <u>cessation</u> of all vital func-
tions: the end of life

You see, they have several meanings, but let's take a closer look at all of them; as we pass by a dark object, it reflects the image of us. Looking at it can be scary, especially in a dark or unfamiliar area; as we are walking by and see our own shadow, we have the intention to jump; that is a frightening experience, not knowing who is lurking around the corner. Now let's say speaking in a metaphor expression we are walking through a valley at night, and we cannot see our way, but seeing shadows can cause frightening that makes us stumble, and can make us fall to our death. Jesus illustrates what the valley of death is like in a spiritual sense.

Matthew 4:16 NIV says the people living in darkness have seen a great light: on those living in the land of the shadow of death, a light has dawned.

This is the prophecy of Christ's coming as a light to the people of Galilee. Christ fulfilled the prophecy by preaching the gospel and revealing God's true meaning to them. With is the light of the world; read Isaiah 9:2.

Isaiah 35;8 <u>New Living Translation</u> stated
And a great road will go through that once deserted land. It will be named the Highway of Holiness. Evil-minded people will never travel on it. It will be only for those who walk in God's ways; fools will never walk there.

Once we believe in Jesus Christ casting all dark-ness away and putting away sin by walking in a spiritual light, darkness must cease. Heaven heard our cry of forgiveness and cleansed us from all unrighteousness. So now we do not have to fear the dark because there is no darkness where light is Jesus.

So, we know the next line said **I will fear no evil,** no evil will entertain the light fear is cast away. **For you are with me** as long as we stay in the body of Christ; which said Jesus is the vine and the believers are the branches, the source of life and nourishment draw from the vine as long as we remain connected to Jesus. Read John 15:51: **Your rod and your staff, they comfort me.** The shepherd defends and protects his sheep from harm in the same way our Father God does for us with comfort and love. Once we put our trust in faith in the all-mighty God we can walk through the valley of the shadow of death and fear no evil because we know you are with us every step of the way and that you will use your rod of correction and your staff for protecting us by comforting us of your grateful love of compassion.

Self-Control
Controlling Domineering Uncontrol

Self-control restraint exercised over one's own impulses, emotions, or desires.

Jesus was an example for us all because he was tempted on all occasions, and he set the bar for controlling our emotions, actions, and feelings. It will bring on destruction. Jesus had the spirit of self-control in him, so it was not hard for him to control his emotions. On the other hand, we, as believers of Christ, can have the same by meditating on his word and by constantly praying in the spirit. Yes, we will be tempted, and that way, we will know how close we are to controlling our emotions. Read the passages below for some clarity.

Philippians 2:13 New International Version for it is God who works in you to will and to act in order to fulfill his good purpose.

Romans 7:21-25 New International Version

> [21] So I find this law at work: Although I want to do good, evil is right there with me. [22] For in my inner being I delight in God's law; [23] but I see another law at work in me, waging war against the law of my mind and making me a prisoner of the law of sin at work within me. [24] What a wretched man I am! Who will rescue me from this body that is subject to death? [25] Thanks be to

God, who delivers me through Jesus Christ our
Lord! So then, I myself in my mind am a slave to
God's law, but in my sinful nature[a] a slave to the
law of sin

**Uncontrol a lack or absence of control tantrum, being unable to
get your way or complaining control the power to influence or
direct people's behavior or the course of events.**

That is something that is not easy to win when you are in the
flesh, your emotions get involved you are straining to not say anything but there it goes you said it. You will say if I only can take it
back, but it is out there in the atmosphere. Even if you're not the
one who bursts out your emotions holding it in and thinking the
worth of that person and not letting the spirit control your thoughts
is just as bad. Your emotions, actions, and feelings still in control.
You are fighting your flesh, and the flesh will always win because it
has no control and must be brought under the spirit's control. Once
the spirit dominates your entire being, every thought will come into
order.

Let's live under the umbrella of the fruit of the spirit: **Love, Joy,
Peace, Patience, Kindness, Goodness Faithfulness, Gentleness,**
and **Self-Control.**

Which the spirit of God controls all. Amen

Purpose

God, we do not want anything from this world if it is not coming from you. We are growing in rich spiritual soil to become the disciples of God, growing and flourishing in his will and having favor with God and man (Proverbs 3:4 KJV). Now your purpose has been fulfilled, and you can go on living the life that God has intended for you to live, a blessed and courageous life on earth. Just imagine the freedom you have walking into God's blessing every day and until he calls us back home.

Prayer

My Heavenly Father, I come to you as humble as I know how. Teach me your will for my life, your purpose, your understanding and ways. Tell me where you want me to go and what you want me to do, and I know I cannot do anything without your help, and I can do nothing unless you guide me through your Holy Spirit. I am leaning, depending on, and trusting you because I know that your word is right and true. Before the world was formed, you spoke it into existence, and we know we can use the same word to speak to our lives. We can do everything through Christ who strengthens us (Philippians 4:13). That's why we call all things forth (Romans 4:17). I am healed by his stripes. I am set free from the bondage of depression, free from anxiety, suicide, free from the bondage of poverty and lack, set free from any kind of demon spirits that try to leak around our homes, our families, our jobs—any area of our lives. We just want to let you know that we love you. We appreciate you. We adore you. We magnify you because of who you are—the Alpha and Omega, the beginning and the ending, wonderful counselor, Almighty God, everlasting father, the Prince of Peace, my provider, my protector. We are grateful because we know you are helping us through our daily walk. Let us be mindful of others. Let us be kind, considerate, and long-suffering to others so we can walk worthily in your statue and be like you. So we thank you in advance because we know everything is working out for our good (Romans 8:28). Amen.

Acknowledgment

I give God all the glory and praise that's due to him.

About the Author

Sharon Gaskin is basing her life on the truth of God's word, "And ye shall know the truth, and the truth shall make you free" (John 8:32 KJV). She was born in San Antonio, Texas. She is a new author writing her first book, *God Is in the Midst of Every Problem*. She enjoys spending time with her family and friends and is a woman of great faith, love, and compassion. She cherishes every moment of sharing God's love. She believes the Bible is an inspiration of God's love for mankind to live by. You are sure to be blessed with her second book, *Living and Growing in the Overflow*, as it guides you through lessons of faith.